NOTHING BUT THE BLOOD

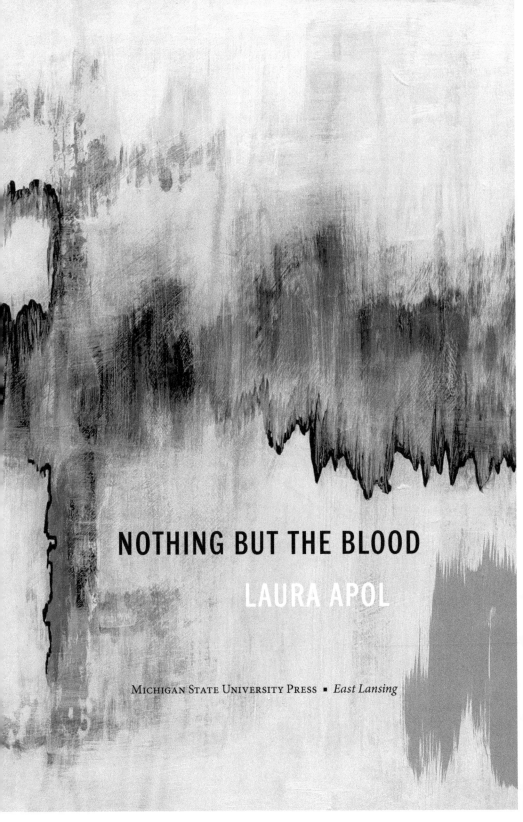

NOTHING BUT THE BLOOD

LAURA APOL

Michigan State University Press ▪ *East Lansing*

♾ The paper used in this publication meets the minimum requirements
of ANSI/NISO Z39.48-1992 (R 1997) (Permanence of Paper).

 Michigan State University Press
East Lansing, Michigan 48823-5245

Printed and bound in the United States of America.

27 26 25 24 23 22 21 20 19 18   1 2 3 4 5 6 7 8 9 10

LIBRARY OF CONGRESS CATALOGING-IN-PUBLICATION DATA
Names: Apol, Laura, 1962- author.
Title: Nothing but the blood / Laura Apol.
Description: East Lansing : Michigan State University Press, [2018]
Identifiers: LCCN 2017058680| ISBN 9781611862997 (pbk. : alk. paper)
| ISBN 9781609175801 (pdf) | ISBN 9781628953459 (epub) | ISBN 9781628963458 (kindle)
Classification: LCC PS3601.P64 A6 2018 | DDC 811/.6—dc23
LC record available at https://lccn.loc.gov/2017058680

Book design by Charlie Sharp, Sharp Des!gns, East Lansing, MI
Cover design by Erin Kirk New
Cover image: clivewa/Adobe Stock

g green press INITIATIVE Michigan State University Press is a member of the Green
Press Initiative and is committed to developing and
encouraging ecologically responsible publishing practices. For more
information about the Green Press Initiative and the use of recycled
paper in book publishing, please visit *www.greenpressinitiative.org.*

Visit Michigan State University Press at *www.msupress.org*

For Hanna
and for Jesse

Because we are linked by blood and blood
is memory without language.

—JOYCE CAROL OATES

CONTENTS

3   On Divine Highway

7   Horoscope

9   Mid-Life

10   Writing the Body

11   The Piano

12   Briars

13   Weeding the Garden with John Calvin

15   Sabbath

16   And then, the Fall

19   Genealogy

20   Colonial History

21   Mother, Smoking

23   Suppose

24   Birthright

27   Midwinter, My Mother

28   Easter Sunday

29   On My Fiftieth Birthday, I Return

30   Motherline

31   Of the Body

32   On Dreams

33   February 29th

37   Sending My Son to College

38   Errant

39   Afterbirth

41   A Photo

42   The Fire

43   Second Sight

44   November Rains

45   Surrender

46   Daughter Leaving Home

49 In the Vineyards of Teramo

52 Blood Moon

53 Caught

54 *Takotsubo*

55 First Peach after the Truth

56 Burning the Old Year

57 Seven Months On

61 Scattering Ashes at Land's End

62 Pardon

63 To the Lighthouse

65 The Gift of *Yes*

66 Roots

67 Five Prayers to Be Said upon Departure

68 Light, Water, Bones

71 On Divine Highway II

73 NOTES

75 ACKNOWLEDGMENTS

NOTHING BUT THE BLOOD

Of obligation
I was taught young:
you will never be able
to pay what you owe.

>   *Oh, how I love Jesus*
>   *because he first loved me.*

But she had just been hurt,
that doe—
red blood, blood-red
leaves on the county road,
sumac on fire.

I wanted her to be saved,
but there was
nothing but the blood
on Divine

—that steaming debt—

and a fawn, wild-eyed
under the weight of sky.

HOROSCOPE

In a past incarnation, it's possible that you were imprisoned
or burned at the stake for expressing your beliefs.
That might help explain why you're sometimes
reluctant to speak your mind with total candor in this life.

Even with the human history of pyre,
every Libra on the planet
cannot previously have been burned.
But never mind the others—for me, the horoscope
is true. I remember those flames.
I've spent half this life avoiding
their return.

Those flames lit my childhood.
The stake was the kitchen chair, where after each fight
my brother and I were set, knee to knee, forced to smile
until our anger was done. My anger never was done,
though I was always the first to be released.

Those flames blazed through my adolescence.
The stake was the passenger seat, where I swooned
and deferred so boys who collected guns
and washed windows at the Co-Op Gas and Oil
would ask me out again.

Those flames raged through my marriage.
The stake was everywhere: the kitchen counter,
dinner table, back yard, double garage. I was a dutiful
wife, keeping cupboards filled, laundry baskets empty,
kneading bread in silence as my resistance rose.

In church, at holiday parties, with the playgroup
in the park: I said I believed what I couldn't,
said I voted for Reagan when I didn't, was silent

when it came to wars, poverty, choice; bit my lip
through jokes about Jews, gays, liberals, and blondes—

never heard my own anger crackling around me,
never noticed the blood in my mouth
tasted of ash.

MID-LIFE

She just wants
to stop being a team player, a good soldier,
someone to count on in a pinch. She wants
to arrive at the meeting unprepared, hair wild,
clothes askew, scent of afternoon sex
and scotch. She wants to wear red stiletto
boots to the dean's brunch, have her tongue
pierced, get a tattoo in a place
everyone can almost see.

She wants
to cancel class for belly dancing,
spend the search committee budget
on a motorcycle tour through the Alps,
get high before the seminar—
powerpoints exploding in a psychedelic haze.
She'll burn job applications in the lobby, one self-
promoting page at a time, place annual reviews
on a blackjack table, bet them all and lose
—for good—the untenable
scourge of words.

She'll celebrate
the slippery slope, the shaking heads,
the cautionary tones. There's a world outside
she wants to take in, a world inside
she just wants to let go.

My mother was always a *no-thank-you*
with her legs crossed. She seldom entertained
possibility. She would have known better

than dinner at nine, settling instead
for a handshake, brief as snow
on warm glass, believing

where there's fire, there's smoke.

But no—words have made me
new. Do you think I have learned
nothing? I doubt that I am someone

you will like. So kiss me now—
we may not cross paths again. Without lipstick,
I look nothing like my mother.

THE PIANO

His hands
hard maple in the rain—
the sheen, the scratches
darkening. The thick wire
veins of his neck, his heart
sticking on, sticking off, the pedal
of his foot rusting

where it rests in the grass. Pooling
in the space between his fingers—
accidentals. My father
thundering *you will regret this
the rest of your life*;
me quitting lessons
because I could.

BRIARS

A friend phones to say her hands are bloody
from thorns, pulling blackberry brambles
at the sides of the drive. They spread,
those tares. My hands, too, are bloody,
but not from uprooting. No,
it is the thicket itself I love, canes
that catch my sleeve; briars buried
in the thin of my wrist. I love the torn
cuffs of the shirt that belonged to my father,
the seeping scrapes, and how I need
to lean into each spine to let it unloose.
So much is embedded in my skin—
the scattered dust of fireflies along the lane,
the heron's wide-winged screech, the church
I left long ago, splintered crossbeams,
and my father's heart on a blue-black
screen, valves that open, close—the press
and push, the largeness and narrows.
Erratic fluttering, jagged thread,
a barb dug deep into my palm—
its stubborn hold.

WEEDING THE GARDEN WITH JOHN CALVIN

We agree on the total depravity
of nettles and nightshade,
the unconditional election
of lavender along the stairs.

But he's inflexible
when I speak of the complexity
of wisteria or Queen Anne's lace,
the original blessing
of raspberry canes.

It's about context and intent,
I explain. *Consider the lily…*

but he has moved on
to limited atonement—
muttering, *Many are called*
but few are chosen as he roots out
the nasturtiums for the fire.

I rush to rescue
the spontaneous sunflowers,
cut their thick stalks.
When he enters the kitchen,
I am arranging them
in a terracotta vase.

He just won't let up:
Is or is not the sunflower made
in the image of God? he persists
as I work. I argue
that even the sunflower
grows weary under everlasting
scrutiny, its petalled head

bowed with the weight
of irresistible grace.

In the end, we both esteem
the perseverance of the sainted
face, the yellow crown—
the seeds that drop
to once again become a weed,

become a flower.

SABBATH

When my grandfather let his field lie fallow
for a season, a decade, even half a lifetime,
he did not plan or predict
what would grow, what would choke,
what would take over or recede;

and when he returned with the plow
to turn the soil in moist and open furrows,
he did not pause to number or name
what he found: ragweed, burdock,
nightshade and shepherd's purse,
volunteer soybeans and corn
—all, beautiful in their surprise and disarray.

I imagine him in the midday heat of the Plains,
wiping sweat as he surveyed
the field behind, the field ahead,
thinking what a good thing rest can be—
thinking how much promise there is
in a field overgrown, and ready.

AND THEN, THE FALL

Salt lick and camo pants,

rifle scope
aimed at the tawny noon.

If you want to believe,
        believe this:

        the aspen grove
no longer shimmers. The grass
        of the field
                has gone bare.

Who watches the sparrow?

Today, every burning bush
        bleeds.

GENEALOGY

After my mother's death, her sisters broke
silence, told of a bloodline
of babies, unspoken:

—still-born, never born,

mis-carried as if they had slipped
through the fingers of the living, lost—
cervine bones along the creekbed.

We didn't talk about such things.

The last story was of Grace,
an aunt none of them had known—

Grace, the youngest, sepia photo
hidden among their mother's things;
clear-eyed Grace, lace collar and finger-
waved hair.

Her siblings kept her secret.

Late December: black ice,
back roads. I wonder which sister
helped button her coat, which brother
drove. Which brother held open
the backstreet side door.

The unstoppable blood.

Once home, who told their mother
about their dying baby sister?

COLONIAL HISTORY

There are stories that are forever
untold. My grandfather's father—

how do I know this?
Before I set foot in the islands,
before I could find them on a map,
I had the word: *Indonesia.*

Was he a soldier? Was he a prisoner?
He was never a wealthy man,
so what are the other options
for this tale?

I cannot avoid the threshold
to the prison under the city hall,
where he crosses into this story—

one side of the metal door
or the other.

They made the ceiling so low
a person could not stand up.
They let the floods come in—
let the rooms fill with terror and tides.

What, then, do I wish for the ending:
that he found himself in rising water

or that he was the one
　　　　　　who'd locked the door?

MOTHER, SMOKING

How could I know that a woman
whose hands could no longer button her blouse
could hold a smoke—hold a smoke till it drops
past the wheels of her chair to the bathroom rug?

How could I know that a woman
whose hands could no longer sign her name
could take a drag—take a drag till it drops
past shoes she is unable to tie?

      *   *   *

That house was filled with smoke—
the holy ghost with yellowed fingers,
blackened lungs, water and wine.

A smoker himself,
my father would not be married
to a woman who would light up. So she swore
she had quit, and he went on buying denial
twenty menthols at a time.

When she was no longer able,
he helped her to the bathroom,
held the Salem to her lips, betrayal
in every draw.

Put out your hand, father. The lit tip
stubbed into your palm is hot as a nail.

      *   *   *

Ash, then, was my inheritance—fallen
from her secret cigarettes, her black-tar affair
of more than fifty years.

This is the blaze that blackens the photos,
me the choked child who tried not to notice
the lipstick-ringed filter in the toilet, prayed
not to smell smoke.

Watch the house burn, child. Watch the split-level
house in flames.

Ashes, ashes. We all fall down.

SUPPOSE

your mother did not die
—suppose she never did,
          your grief gone,
pollen in the breeze. Suppose
she said your name

this time. Suppose
your father, then, didn't turn
          to you
to fix his world. Suppose
he looked up

from his broken mirror,
saw the wild
          fish—your stippled stripes,
the flash of fin. Suppose
you never carried

in your natal cells the ache
of all your parents could not
          bear. You would not need
to read the room,
          the clock, each face,
                    to find yourself.

BIRTHRIGHT

Saturdays, my mother
took me to her mother:

rose patterns on china, dish towels
cross-stitched with days of the week;
a rat-tailed comb, brush curlers,
pink hair-set tape, and Dippity-Do.

I dusted mopboards,
shook rugs and polished silver
while my mother, stiff with silence,
washed and styled her mother's hair.

The house smelled of setting gel,
rose water and rage—ghost tongues
weary of their stories.

Decades later, my daughter
learned to polish
my mother's nails; I buttoned
her blouse, teased her hair.
Each visit bore the tarnish
of never-enough.

Now I live alone by a river.
My daughter seldom calls;
I rarely answer.
Only the salmon return
each autumn, doubling back
to the stream they were born in.

Along the banks, cattails explode
—a thousand furred tongues.

MIDWINTER, MY MOTHER

After I left the cemetery, I drove—
east to the ocean, seven states away.
The journey was slow, weighted as I was,
myself in my arms. I thought
she would go with me. I thought
she would stay with me in my sleep. Instead,
I dreamed of fallen horses, ruins of battle
—those useless limbs, those dying horses'
eyes. I walked on the beach
until I understood: how time and water
grind down the world, hand us our cartilage,
broken. Hand us our bones.
She'd understood, in the end,
because I had to tell her. I stood by her bed,
kept my mind on the moon, the clear
winter light. I wanted to hear her say
she loved me, and I pretended she did,
pretended to hear those words in the waves—
above shards of shell, fish bones
picked clean.

EASTER SUNDAY

I knew she would come to me in the spring,
not as a heron or owl or steady cardinal flame,

but as a flash, years in the making—a moment
my hunger could not afford to miss.

And so I put out feeders, bulging with seed.
It was the year everything bloomed

too soon or not at all, the year
of extravagant finches: I couldn't get over

how yellow they flew. When the calico
brought gilded feathers to the door,

I knew what I loved was truly gone.
Still, those feathers littering the steps

were not without grace, which meant
I could love the finch—frail, electric petals

of light. But I could love, too, the cat,
taking and giving in equal measure,

and those vivid feathers, warm in my palm.

The street, the market,
the church on the corner—how can I turn back
the trees? There would have been
leaves, this yellow, and light, and the same
October air. A woman rose that day, felt
the stretch of her skin and a baby's kick,
breasts tender, back swayed. These motes in the air:
is this all that remains? The body that held me
is gone; brick-solid, the garage apartment
where she slept and woke. These sills
hold that morning: her breath at the window,
her bent-double prayers. The stoop
where she stood, the stained concrete steps—
how can I turn back the sky?

MOTHERLINE

The veins on your legs
are your motherline, a blue umbilicus
stretching from your grandmother
through your mother
to the thick purple blossoms
on the curves of your calves, indigo
tendrils, violet bouquets,
and the only day the doctors
can laser them invisible
is the third Wednesday of October,
—your mother's birth day, grief
the hot needle searing to scars
the flowers you would place on a table,
a hospital bedside, a grave.

OF THE BODY

A she-bear comforts me in the morning
two years after my mother's death, climbs
onto the shabby sofa of my childhood,
covers me with heavy limbs, warm breath. I lie
still beneath her. It is winter, wind
howling down the chimney, the fire
cold. The river has broken

into large floes that drift downstream,
ice buckling onto itself, all fissures and folds.

*   *   *

My mother never wanted to be buried
in frozen ground, but at the cemetery
we had to make our way across drifts, gullies

of snow, hunched against the wind. Is it true
believers are buried with their feet to the east,

so when they are raised they face Christ, the risen
sun? I picture her now, a Sunday school painting—
suddenly upright, face alight, frozen earth
ruptured and falling away.

*   *   *

All week, I have looked for an eagle circling.
The skies are silent. There are deer,
and the tracks of deer. A lone fox.
And an ice bird on the snow—russet wings,
a wild tuft and ruddy beak.

Open the window. Let the red bird in.

ON DREAMS

You start to recognize animals
by their stance, by their walk,
by their wing strokes in the winter sky:
this is an osprey, this a hawk; those wings
are a heron, an eagle; that blue flash, a jay.

You start to recognize history, too, by its trace—
cellular memories that appear in your sleep:
this is my seared vein, my father's
drowned macula; and here is my mother—
her hands and her smile.

She looks so good. And to think
we thought she was going to die.

The snow arrives at dawn,
        white on white:
smoke from the woodstove,
ice on the river. All day

I watch for you. Four years,
the leap of time
        from your death
to this day. Then, too, snow

obscured the picture—
        mother-in-my-mind
with whom it would take decades
to make peace.

But I want a sign.
        I want a sign
that things are right with us now.
I want to believe

        in an afterlife
where you hold out
your arms to me,
        wide as the wings

of the swan I am not able to see
until, from the white river
it soars
into the storm
        of this blinding day.

The terrier we adopted is afraid of folded newspapers and men in caps. The blue-eyed cat from the Rescue is terrified of roads and cars, and can't stop eating, even when there is enough. History is told through what is feared and what is craved. Nineteen years growing a boy into a man, stories like tree rings circling a heart that once beat within me, and today he steps from this familiar world to his next, several states away. So little difference between *love* and *lose*. He stands near the car, wearing a pack and a hat. The dog approaches his outstretched hand with caution; the cat watches from a distance as he drives away. I feel the space in me grow, hollow as I was in the days after his birth, when my stretched skin was too large for my emptied-out body; my breath, too small.

ERRANT

The teen-aged daughter
who last night reminded me
I know nothing about anything,
            and most of all nothing about her,

this morning decided
I might know something after all.
I might know where her earring landed
when it fell as she ran distance
yesterday after school.

No ordinary charm—
a gift just that morning from the first boy
to give her a token of any sort.
I imagine him, half her height,
holding out the small blue box;
imagine her smile, her pleasure, all that light.

So I find myself
in the field behind her school
searching the chill for one errant earring,
as if she might be right and a mother *can* intuit
where a sterling hoop lies hidden in the grass.
It is the first morning of frost,
and every blade is stiff,
            silver-white and shining.

I pace the edge of the field
with measured steps,
            —forward, back—
scanning for silver against the rising sun,
thinking of my daughter as she runs—
her lean strong legs,
            her tangled white-blond hair.

AFTERBIRTH

I wake in the dark to a full morning
moon. My daughter's eighteenth birthday,
and I am bleeding, as I did
in the days after she was born.
Now, as then, my empty womb contracts.

Outside her room, I pause
to hear her breathe, even and steady,
think of the ways she has shared
my blood: all I tried to give her,
all I could not keep her from

—the way I told time before her birth
(in five moons, the baby will be born;
in two moons, the baby will be born)

—my shuffling walks
down hospital hallways, infant
in my arms, as I murmured,
I have a daughter, I have a daughter.

Her father and I vied for her
from the start, each of us wanting
the woman she would become. She started
her cycles linked to mine—two women
tuned to the same lunar score, her young body
following, then eclipsing my own.

When, on his yearly visits, her father
tried to blunt her blossoming, she turned
her rage on me: wanting, not wanting
to be home; wanting, not wanting
to be held.

So I sit on the porch in the early
hush, sifting our splintered past. Nearby,
a nightbird cries, and I step to the door.
There, in the arms of the elm, a dark bundle:
Great Horned Owl—

such insistent calls, such loud silence
in between. From her perch, she spreads
her wide-shadow wings, catches
the breaking light and—rising—
blots out the blood-red dawn.

A PHOTO

My daughter is off to her last day of school, *ever*. In her miniskirt and heels, eyes rimmed black, lips red, she is all about her missing calculus book, pack hoisted to her shoulder as she marches out, rejecting even this moment of ritual: each fall, first day of school—photo on the porch; each spring, last day of school—photo on the porch. Thirteen years should mean thirteen pairs of photos, now less one. I picture the shots in a line, season in, season out, everything a blur between—my failures, glyphs in her growing bones, in the cells of her changing hair and baby-to-permanent teeth, the prints growing clearer each year. Her dreams faltered long ago, her world harsher than I imagined, and we have—each of us—paid. So this morning offers no porch smile, no bitter-sweet tears. No click of a shutter—just a door slammed shut.

THE FIRE

*When you do something, you should burn yourself
completely, like a good bonfire, leaving no trace.*
—SHUNRYU SUZUKI

I draw solace from this solitude,

the labyrinth of desert grass and dried
creek beds, the absolution
of the morning stars. Here, the world
forgives—

until my distant daughter
rises from the hard red dirt, wings
white with ash. She reels me
in on the taut umbilical of care:

*why didn't you why can't you why won't you
love me?* And then my own, *how could I
not?*

Once, I mapped the moons
toward when she would be born

until she broke the membrane
of my stretched embrace, emerged
hand-first. Even then she could not wait
to leave.

Now her rage consumes us;
flinted words throw sparks, savage fingers
flare. She points her fury
across miles and years and

—tinder that I have become—for her,
I burn.

SECOND SIGHT

The first time it happened, my son
was two and we were at the Food Lion:
I turned from him to choose onions,

potatoes for supper, and when I turned back,
a strange woman had called him by name.
He was lit up—*Pam!*—and with that word a rift
appeared and I saw, whole, the life he would learn
that was not me: komodo dragons,
the state motto of Oklahoma, how glass
is blown, the way the melody inverts
in a fugue. *Muscle memory deserts you first,*

he would say as his fingers found notes
I never knew. *The Perseids peak before dawn,* and
Always lead with the knight. His worlds unfurled
beyond my sight: the Greek island of Syros,
the mountain temples of Nepal.
And this morning he saw the sun rise,
the full moon set from the summit
of Mt. Whitney, apex of the Western Divide.

Here, leaves pour down in a honeyed rain;
my midnight sky is curtained by clouds.
A lone swan drifts on the river of my sleep.

NOVEMBER RAINS

If my daughter were here, I would
walk with her into this grey and heartless
day, show her where a half-moon
curve of woven grass is cradled
in the crook of the oak, or sheltered
beneath the eaves. A nest can withstand
wind, and winter, I would say. It waits,
upturned—a begging hand.

SURRENDER

attachment is the root of suffering
—GAUTAMA BUDDHA

You walk up Borobudur in silence,
circling each level of the temple sunwise
three times. It is a lesson

in cut stone, in carvings,
in bell-shaped *stupas* that point the way
to heaven, each step a practice

in loosening desire.
The guide says on the seventh level
you can make your personal request

for blessing. You circle and climb. Circle
and climb. With each footfall,
you hold your daughter

in your mind. Yesterday, at the Pièta,
you lit a candle; tomorrow,
you will cover your head,

bare your feet in the mosque.
You are desperate
for an ear that is listening.

Like the saffron-robed monks who bow
with each breath, with each step
you hold
                    and let go.

DAUGHTER LEAVING HOME

I love the word *fragile*, love
    the word *tensile*—

and how, in stretching, some things
are both. Some things

        are not.

Once on windy Bowen,
I saw a spider's web—

            spun silk
        buoyed between branchings,

            shining wet
        with end-of-summer dew—

and tried to fix it
in a photo.   With just the breath
of my approach

it ruined.

        What am I saying, then?

The late fields are yellowing. Here
and there,   a leaf turns.

Each hummingbird
      may be the season's last

—so much distance
      in a sky this blue.

IN THE VINEYARDS OF TERAMO

—for Franco

You are named for the man
who told you stories
of the vineyards of his youth

when you, too, were learning
the ways of love. There was the sun.
There was the light.

There were the vines and grapes,
the thick spread of honey
across breasts, belly and thighs,

and the gift of pleasure
a man can give and taste
in a woman's skin.

It was a fine-grained photo
of his life, oceans ago—
your grandfather creating with words

the land he had left and the man
he had been, carrying love
on his tongue for the rest of his years.

*   *   *

We will know it together, someday—
that Adriatic light, the lush vines
covering the hillsides of Abruzzo,

and the hum of bees
threaded through the sweet smell
of ripening fruit.

And when at last
we lie down in that vineyard,
the echo of grapes in the air,

I will call you by the name
you and he share—the name of a man
who passed on

the pleasures of skin and tongue,
the sweetness of light,
and the warm honeyed taste of Teramo.

*   *   *

Say this is the place, these
the hillsides your grandfather
wandered, the thick vines he loved.

Picture his stained fingers
turning these tendrils,
these blossoms and shoots.

By night, we take the fruit,
breathe in its color, roll its velvet
names on our tongues:

Montepulciano d'Abruzzo,
Pepe Trebbiano, vintage *Aurora*—
the complex palate

of a wine-maker's dream. By day, too,
we sample the vines, live into the story
you learned long ago:

clay lime soil at my back, Gran Sasso peaks
and thunder in the distance—
the sky opening as I unlock your name.

And so we are soaked by Abruzzi rain,
here in the vineyards that speak to you
of home, and passion quickening

across continents and time.
Say this is the sweetness
your grandfather savored—

you, the future
he pressed himself toward.

BLOOD MOON

These days, our world is stained red:

the Revlon polish I purchase on impulse;
Mars, the rogue planet we pursue, top down,
along empty gravel roads; crimson sheets
and the heat of a late summer moon.

If I asked, I'm sure you would tell me
what I want to know: where does love go?
and how soon does it return?

For years I have prized cardinals,
their unapologetic brightness, pure song.
When the cat crosses the yard,
mouth scarlet with feathers,

I think I have wanted too much
something so fragile, something
with wings: love—all timing and color.
My ruby nails flame.

CAUGHT

I do not recognize the woman
in his doorway,
          watching us sleep.

I do not recognize the mirror
in the pain, truth
          a naked eye, a polished hook.

Such a blinding world for gills.
Like dories dashed up on the deck,
          we gasp—

TAKOTSUBO

Except the lilies,
except the vase, which was shattered,
except the torn photos, crushed shells,

he thinks it can be the same-—

his lover in the doorway,
Basho's short-lived summer moon.

And the octopus trapped in a pot
and the pot in the cave of the ocean,
takotsubo:

      the stunned heart stopping itself.

Four arms, four legs intertwined—

except the hollow muscle of the dream,
except the venae cavae tentacles,
except the unglazed lair—

the autumn ruin.

FIRST PEACH AFTER THE TRUTH

You held the cyanide stone
in your hand—a pitted
promise, rutted
prayer—planted it
deep in history's sudden
ash. A cover of leaf
mold. Winter
rains. You forgot
what was buried there,
later offered me the flesh
of that bitter fruit,
called it a gift. I tasted
blood: the iron-red
veins, rust on my tongue.

BURNING THE OLD YEAR

So much of any year is flammable

—NAOMI SHIHAB NYE

I cannot get the fire in the grate to catch—time and again, the paper's edge glows red, goes out. Across the country, mountain ranges burn by chance; cities, too—billboards, porch swings, children's toys reduced to ash. Like the pregnant woman, heartsick, who does not want a child, telling her story to the woman who each month longs to conceive; like the farmer, field dying from drought, praying to the same god who sends floods to his brother three states away. Mangoes rot on the forest floor; corn left in the field goes to the deer. Tonight, check-stubs, dried flowers, tickets and coat-claims all smoke but will not blaze. Your name, though—it throws sparks. I blow, steady, on the pyre.

The mole the cat brought home
seeps blood, a heart-shaped
stain on the step. I search
the grass for the finch
that hit the bedroom
glass. Such a fascination
with endings: the way the dog
rushes each morning to learn
whether what died in the woods
is still dead. The way in France,
a whole town gathered around
a piece of star

that fell to a field. And how,
with coffee, I look out
at the sycamores—mottled
apparitions against autumn grey.
I wonder if there's something
wrong, what is able to survive.
How much, really, do I wish?
Bleached skeletons
without bark, limbs empty
and inviting—

place, now,
for the river hawk to roost.

SCATTERING ASHES AT LAND'S END

—FOR JEAN

I wish I had written these words
before I was carrying ash.
I do not want to walk where we walked
stand where we stood
with nothing but ashes in hand.

I should have written lines to capture your glee
as you drove the countryside's narrow roads,
hedgerows scraping the car, greeting oncoming drivers
with a wave and *Carry on, old chap!*—
recorded our talk over bangers and mash,
Guinness and chips, sloe Plymouth gin.

All right then, you would intone,
British as could be, as if everything *were* all right
—as if neither of us saw the sword raised over your head,
as if we could wish our way into a future,
year after improbable year. *Cheers, mate.*
Let's become old women together.

I want you to take in this harbor, this English mist,
these moors and the dark Notter pub,
lead me again on a bike through the city,
insist if I don't buy the painting,
I'll live with regret. I bought it that day;
where's the guarantee on regret?

I want you to raise your children, love your man,
rise from the dust in my hand
to lift a glass to our good health, good luck.
We've got it all, luv, you would tell me once more.
Your bones, ground to memory, cling to my skin.

PARDON

We are months into silence
and I have brewed a single cup of tea.

The patio feeder holds the remnants
of seeds placed to lure songbirds
to the yard. This summer, a swarm
of yellowjackets took over. I meant
to get rid of them, empty the seed,
spray the hive. The feeder's glass
frames the fine paper folds of their nest.

I recall the springtime orioles we courted
with syrup—the one that hit the pane
and fell, stunned, to the grass; the pair
of turkey vultures nested high on the beam
of the barn. You urged me to greet
their auspicious arrival, welcome their daily
returns. I drove them away,

chose instead wild geese in flight—
the spread of their V in the sky
and the way, before I could stay
their sound, they were gone.
Today, their September shadows
once more cross the yard—a fringed
span of endings, winter to come.

Only the yellowjackets remain,
a brief autumn reprieve. I cradle
my cooling cup, consider once more
the feeder where wasps
hover and hum, thin-winged,
graceful as any hollow-boned bird.

TO THE LIGHTHOUSE

Ghosts always listen for their names.
—WENDY MORTON

On this shipwreck coast of Superior,
there are ghosts enough—lost souls
ascending from the deep,

in love once more with the light.
You hiked here long ago
with the woman who was then your wife,

and the lighthouse that draws us on
is the one you climbed.
It couldn't save every ship.

The water-soaked ribs
of boats that sank near the shore
gleam in the afternoon hours,

slick-timbered ladders from the sea.
We work to navigate the edges
of this perilous past,

these icy waters, this graveyard
studded with shoal.
Love has so little chance.

As always, I fill my pockets
one stone at a time
—jasper, granite, agate, quartz—

while you point out cold currents,
salmon runs, proof
stories never change—

each wild fish
lives only to find the plume of the river,
forge upstream its solitary return.

I hear once more the siren songs
luring sailors, luring women
into the waves. Turning,

I lay the smooth stones at my feet.

THE GIFT OF *YES*

I tell my mother I want to
go to the lake, waterskiing with friends,
instead of to Sunday service

and this time she does not say,
      Laura, you know how we feel about this.

She does not say,
      You can make up your own mind.
      But you know how we feel about this.

She does not say,
      My parents would never have let me go,
      but you can make up your own mind.
      And you know how we feel about this.

Instead, she says,
      Yes. Have a good time. And here's some money
      for ice cream—

and in that moment
her own father opens the car door,
her mother hands me suntan lotion and a hat,
her sister tosses me a towel,

and with her gift of *yes,* my mother
climbs in beside me in the back.

ROOTS

You phoned Sunday
to say your younger brother had died.

I tried to read your voice the way I read the river,
heard underneath
a story you'd told me last summer
—how, as a child you studied the roads
when your family went for a drive, learning
the landmarks

so that if your parents left you,
you could find the way back.
You were the firstborn.
It would be up to you to lead the others home.

Today your family will gather once more—
dark suits, white roses. For me, you have laid out
the family tree: great uncles, second cousins,
a tangle of generations.

But I see only that backseat boy
who watched out the Buick's side window,
thinking about routes,

knelt for first communion at the rail at St. Bart's
wearing the welt of the razor strop,

who in a few hours will cross himself, kneel again
before something he no longer believes, lay to rest
a hope he can no longer carry

—a boy who never will make his way home.

FIVE PRAYERS TO BE SAID UPON DEPARTURE

—for Rich

With us it was always the ocean—
its rhythm the backdrop of all we did.
So how did I not know the day you died,
bent as I was toward the sea,
handing your story to whichever gods
listen? And then the morning after:
on the beach each bit of coral
was shaped like a brain.
The shells were shards
of a heart—I wished to hold
each to my ear. So the boats go out,
the boats come in, and if my soul
were not so moored to this world
I would ride the taste of salt
far from the shore—you, the night bird
beside the hull, just clearing the wake.
Somewhere, someone is playing Cohen's
Hallelujah, drinking Jameson
neat. Tonight, I'll light a candle,
set it afloat. The moon pulls the tide
even when there is no light to see.

LIGHT, WATER, BONES

On the far bank, a willow weeps,
while in the river, its mirror
ripples with light. The cloud-blemished sky
meets a perfect dappling beneath.

Here are Plato's images in reverse,
the ideal in the darkening current:

a leaf, a branch, an evening bat.
Even the heron steps gently,
afraid to startle the flawless
heron at its feet.

Along the lane, the deer carcass
does not teach me about life or death,
but about the curve of ribs
whitening under the moon.

The lessons I learn
are soundless: the light, the water,
the delicate bleach of bones.

After years of listening,
perhaps in my next life
I will not need to learn to trust—

will come back faithful
to my own sense of smell,
wander like the possum, solitary,
through the night brush and broken limbs,

burrow fearless as the sleek black mole,
far from this world's polished
surface, intimate with the wet
roots of things.

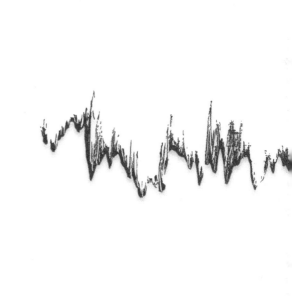

She had just been hurt,
that doe—
red blood, blood-red
leaves on the county road,
sumac on fire.

I wanted her to be saved,
but there was nothing—

nothing but the blood.

NOTES

PAGE vii. Joyce Carol Oates, *I Lock my Door upon Myself* (New York: Ecco Press, 1990), 85.

PAGE 13. The five points of Calvin's doctrines are as follows: total depravity, unconditional election, limited atonement, irresistible grace, perseverance of the saints.

PAGE 53. Borobudur is the world's largest Buddhist temple, located in Central Java, Indonesia. The Pièta is in Gereja Santa Perawan Maria Diangkat Ke Surga (The Church of Our Lady of Assumption) in Jakarta; directly across the street from this cathedral was built the Istiqlal (Independence) Mosque, the largest mosque in Southeast Asia.

A *stupa* is a Buddhist commemorative mound usually containing holy relics; the upper levels of Borobudur have a total of 72 bell-shaped stupas, many still containing a statue of the Buddha partly visible through the perforated stonework. During the Vesak ceremony, which occurs once a year during a full moon, thousands of saffron-robed Buddhist monks walk in solemn procession to Borobudur to observe the Buddha's birth, death, and enlightenment.

PAGE 65. Takotsubo cardiomyopathy, also known as "broken-heart syndrome," occurs when, under periods of extreme stress, the heart appears as the shape of the *takotsubo*—the octopus pot in Japan, where it was first described.

ACKNOWLEDGMENTS

I am grateful this past year for the loving presence and support of so many people—I cannot begin to name them here. I will not even try; the list would go on and on. Instead, I express heartfelt thanks to those who held and shaped these poems, though sometimes caring about the poems and caring about the poet were one in the same. I know I will have overlooked some individuals; I apologize in advance. Please know that my heart is grateful, even if my memory is flawed.

In no particular order, then, I wish to thank: Carol Mason-Straughan, Roxanne Klauka, Melanie Morrison, Stephanie Alnot, Stephanie Jordan, and Ron May for your years of listening, reading, and ongoing encouragement; Ruelaine Stokes, for your tireless efforts to keep poetry happening in mid-Michigan, and Joyce Benvenuto, the most enthusiastic poet I know; Cynthia Hockett, for believing poetry actually *is* part of your job description; Scott Harris and that wonderful independent bookstore, Everybody Reads, where I am celebrated as the kind of poet I can only dream of becoming; Rena Upitis, a wise woman, great-hearted friend, the force behind Wintergreen, and someone I can never admire enough; and all the Wintergreen workshop participants—thank you for letting me be an honorary Canadian, year after year. Many thanks to the Michigan State University Press: Gabriel Dotto, Director, and Kristine Blakeslee, Managing Editor; once again, it has been a pleasure to work with your remarkable team. To Lorna Crozier—I cannot imagine a more talented and generous mentor, cheerleader, friend. What grace to find you at just the right moment, so many times. And to David Pimm. When words fail me, you always have them. Thank you.

My deepest gratitude is to my parents, Dallas and Gladys Apol. I grew up in a particular world, at a particular time, and I am forever grateful for the solid loving grounding I received. I could not be the person I am without it. To Jesse—time and again, you inspire and amaze. And to Hanna. Always.

* * *

Several of these poems have been previously published in the following journals and anthologies, sometimes in earlier versions or with a different title:

JOURNALS: "Midwinter, My Mother" in *The Briar Cliff Review*; "Briars" in *Medical Literary Messenger*; "Five Prayers to Be Said upon Departure," "Genealogy," "Second Sight," "*Takotsubo*" in *Nimrod International Journal*; "Light, Water, Bones," "On My Fiftieth Birthday, I Return," "Roots," "Seven Years On" in *Sixfold*.

ANTHOLOGIES: "Five Prayers to be Said upon Departure," "Light, Water, Bones" (as "In My Next Life"), "Midwinter, My Mother," "On Divine Highway," "On My Fiftieth Birthday, I Return," "Second Sight," "Suppose," "*Takotsubo*" in *Coyotes: Tucson Festival of Books Literary Awards*; "Horoscope" in *Embers and Flames*; "Afterbirth," "Errant," "The Fire" in *Imagine This: An Artprize Anthology 2013*; "Easter Sunday" in *Imagine This: An Artprize Anthology 2014*; "In the Vineyards of Teramo," "Sending My Son to College" in *Imagine This: An Artprize Anthology 2015*; "Weeding the Garden with John Calvin" in *Momma's Prayer Flags: A Wintergreen Anthology*; "To the Lighthouse" in *Poems from Planet Earth*; "Horoscope" in *Prairie Gold: An Anthology of the American Heartland*; "Mid-Life" in *Syracuse Cultural Workers' Women Artists Datebook*; "Daughter Leaving Home" in *Teasing the Tongue: A Wintergreen Anthology*.

A number of these poems also have appeared in the chapbooks *Celestial Bodies* (Leaf Press, 2016) and *With a Gift for Burning* (Finishing Line Press, 2018).